CRF 08/21

Please return this book on or before the date shown above. To renew go to www.essex.gov.uk/libraries, ring 0345 603 7628 or go to any Essex library.

D1369048

3013030169241 3

CONTENTS

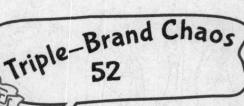

Know the Ropes

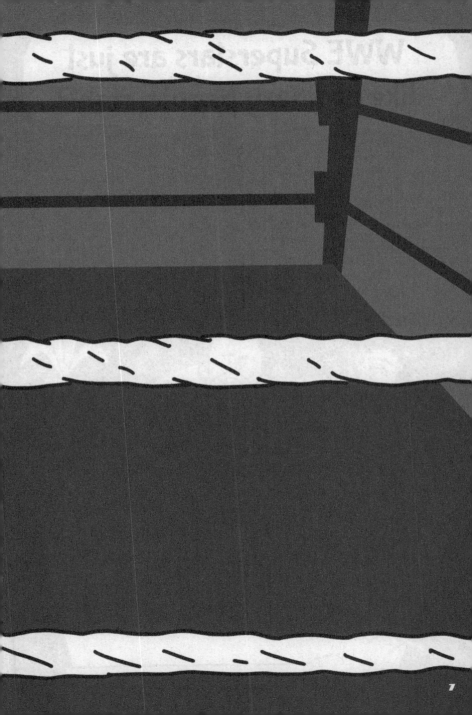

WWE Superstars are just like ordinary people, right?

Just like us ordinary folk, WWE Superstars all have to eat, sleep, get from **A to B**, look after their families and… uhh… watch TV. But of course, they do tend to live life on a larger scale than the average person does.

And they might sometimes do things in a slightly more **"super"** way than the rest of us, even when they are away from the ring.

"Now, where can those car keys be?"

Why is it called a ring when it's square?

Hundreds of years ago wrestlers fought inside a circle drawn on the ground. When wrestling became an organised sport, they started fighting inside a specially built square arena. But for some reason the name **"ring"** stuck.

I say there you Lubberwort, I will not doff my hat to you!

The ring measures **122 metres** (20 × 20 feet). It's built from wooden planks and steel beams. Each side has four ropes, attached to the corner posts by padded turnbuckles.

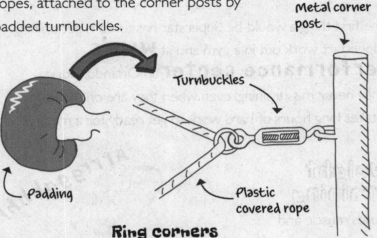

Ring corners

It's also covered by a canvas mat with plenty of padding underneath. That padding is **very important**.

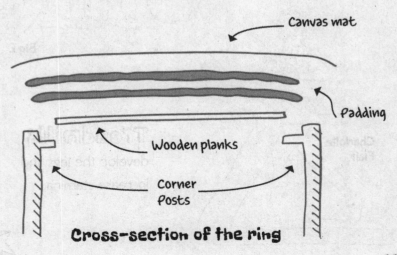

Cross-section of the ring

Training

The first thing a would-be Superstar has to do is get training.
Superstars work out in a gym and at **WWE'S
Performance Center** in Orlando, Florida.
They never miss training, even when they are on the road.
It takes long hours of hard work to get ready for a match,

Weight training

builds muscle and
upper body strength.

Arrrggghhh!

Big E

Charlotte
Flair

Treadmills

develop the legs and
increase stamina.

Where do Superstars train?

New competitors train to become sports entertainment stars at the WWE Performance Center. The center has everything an athlete needs to be come a WWE Superstar.

Talking trash

A Superstar is more than just an athlete – they're a performer, too. At the WWE Performance Center, Superstars record messages for their rivals, baiting them before a match with a stream of insults.

Kevin Owens

Anybody who doesn't know who I am quite frankly is not worth my time.

Dress for success

Any self-respecting Superstar wants to grab the audience's attention from the moment they enter the ring. This is where ring gear comes in.

Charlotte Flair makes sure all eyes are on her with a wardrobe of **DRAMATIC**, wide-sleeved robes.

? ? ?

What kind of mask will **Rey Mysterio** appear in next? It's a **mystery** until he steps into the ring.

? ?

You might need to put your shades on when the **New Day** appear in their ⟍⟍⟍⟍⟍⟍⟍ **eye-popping** ⟋⟋⟋⟋⟋⟋⟋ colors!

Bianca Belair sews her own ring gear. It usually has **Sequins** because "Superstars are meant to shine!"

You can say that again!

Word up! A punchy catchphrase or motto is a must for any sports entertainment star. If a Superstar repeats their catchphrase often, they will soon have their fans chanting it back at them.

Roman Reigns

Believe that!

Braun Strowman

Get these hands!

Crews can't lose!

Apollo Crews

I am the man!

Becky Lynch

Feel the glow!

I'm awesoooooome!

Naomi

The Miz

Of course, there's nothing to stop a Superstar from having **more than one catchphrase**...

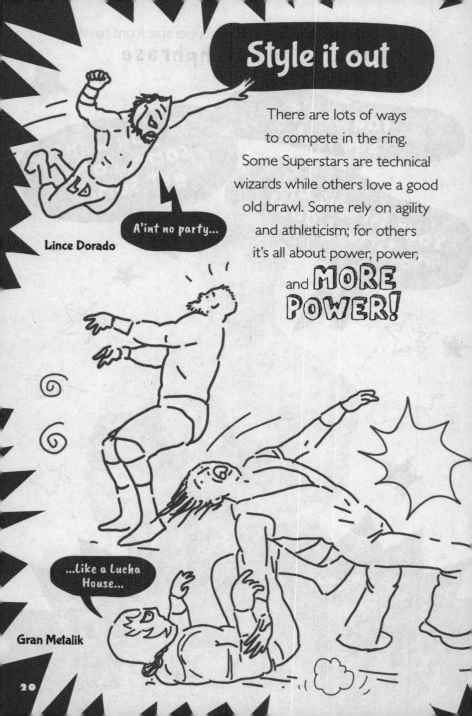

Style it out

There are lots of ways to compete in the ring. Some Superstars are technical wizards while others love a good old brawl. Some rely on agility and athleticism; for others it's all about power, power, and **MORE POWER!**

A'int no party...

Lince Dorado

...Like a Lucha House...

Gran Metalik

Montez Ford of the Street Profits specialises in **flying**... or at least, he jumps so high he looks like he is flying.

Kalisto

...PARTY!

The best Superstars work to develop a style that's all their own. Every time Lucha House Party appear, the ring becomes one huge **riot** of quickfire moves and airborne action.

Playing tag

A tag team is a combination of two or more Superstars competing against another team of two or more Superstars. Only one member of each team is allowed in the ring at a time. When they want to swap places, the Superstar in the ring "tags", or touches, a teammate outside.

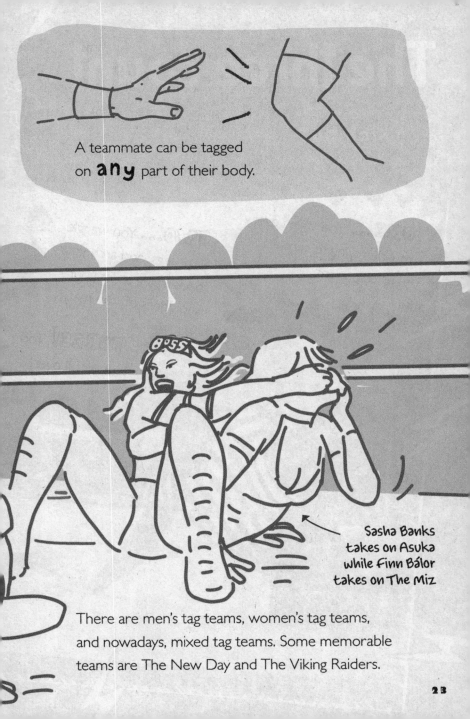

A teammate can be tagged on **any** part of their body.

Sasha Banks takes on Asuka while Finn Bálor takes on The Miz

There are men's tag teams, women's tag teams, and nowadays, mixed tag teams. Some memorable teams are The New Day and The Viking Raiders.

The three count

When pinned down by an opponent, a Superstar must "**kick out**" within the referee's count of three to avoid defeat.

ONE... You strain every muscle trying to remove your opponent...

TWO... You waggle your legs and arch your back trying to lift your shoulders off the mat...

THREE! Too bad, it's all over!

ONE, TWO, THREE!

T-Bar pins Ricochet at the RAW ThunderDome

The thrill of victory

For a Superstar, there's no thrill like the thrill of victory — that magic moment when the referee raises their hand aloft in the middle of the ring. Who cares if it was by **pin**, **knockout**, or **submission**?

Bobby Lashley

Winner Winner Chicken dinner!

That deafening roar isn't the sound of adrenalin pounding through the winner's veins. It's the cheers of the crowd, known in WWE as the **WWE Universe**. Soak it up, Superstar — you showed them who is best!

Make Your Match

Just bring it!

Not all WWE matches are straight-up one-on-one battles. There's a whole range of different matches with different rules, involving different numbers of Superstars and different ring set-ups. Some of them use props, too!

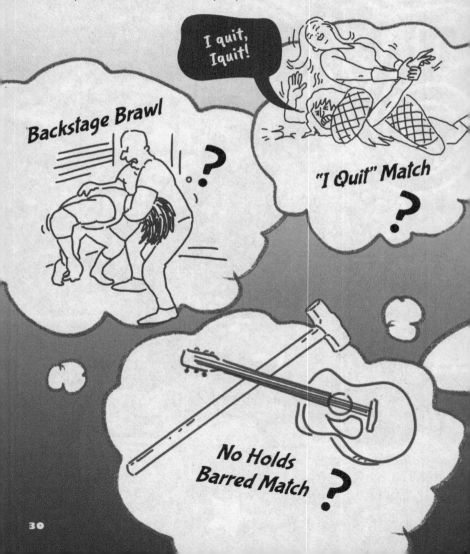

I quit, I quit!

Backstage Brawl ?

"I Quit" Match ?

No Holds Barred Match ?

Take your pick and make your match!

Money in the Bank Match

?

TLC Match ?

Iron Man :10 MATCH?

Regular matches

A regular match is as straightforward as it gets. Two Superstars go at each other, aiming to win by either pinning their opponent or trapping them in such a painful hold that they have to submit by "tapping out." OUCH!

Natalya

TAP TAP TAP

No cheating!

Cheating can result in disqualification. Low blows and using an illegal weapon are **NOT ALLOWED**.

There are dozens of different moves a Superstar can use on their opponent. The **POWER SLAM** is one of them. Braun Strowman uses this move to disable his foes. Like all the moves, it's very dangerous unless you have proper training.

So **DON'T** even think about trying it at home!

Braun Strowman

Don't try this at home, kids!

Pinned down

Keith Lee

Braun Strowman

Kevin Owens

Otis

Sheamus

Seth Rollins

Survivor Series

In a Survivor Series Match, teams of **five** Superstars battle it out in a marathon tag team contest. It's not hard to believe that these matches can go on for some time. In the 2016 *Survivor Series*, one match lasted for nearly **53** minutes.

Riddle

Nia Jax

Natalya

King Corbin

The Superstars in each team represent their WWE brands – **RAW** or **SmackDown**. After battle commences, one member at a time is eliminated until an entire team is left with no members. In other words, **no survivors**.

We take NO SURVIVORS!

Yeah!

Left: Nia Jax, Mickie James, Tamina, and Bayley. Right: Asuka, Naomi, Sonya Deville, and Mandy Rose, Survivor Series 2018

Not all Survivor Series Matches are 5 on 5. Sometimes teams of up to **10** are pitted against each other!

TLC Matches

Did you think TLC meant "tender loving care"? Not always! In the world of WWE it means **"Tables, Ladders, and chairs"**.

Nearly there... nearly...

In a TLC match, Superstars use these household items to help them reach a **prize** suspended above the ring.

Aleister Black

Of course this is WWE, so Superstars also use the tables, ladders, and chairs in all kinds of creative ways. They are useful for **blocking** opponents, **striking** them, or for **jumping** off to take down an opponent with a flying leap.

Triple Threat and Fatal 4–Way Matches

Sometimes, it takes more than two to make a magnificent match. A Triple Threat Match has three Superstars battling it out in the ring. A Fatal 4-Way has (you guessed it) four. These are exciting matches because the first person to get a pin gets the win!

Jeff Hardy, AJ Styles, and Sami Zayn battle in a Triple Threat Match on SmackDown.

It's entirely possible for a Superstar to lose the match without being pinned themselves. All it takes is for one of their opponents to pin another, and everyone else is out. That's why it's called **"fatal"**.

All dressed up and I hardly got a touch!

Kayden Carter

Paige

Money in the Bank

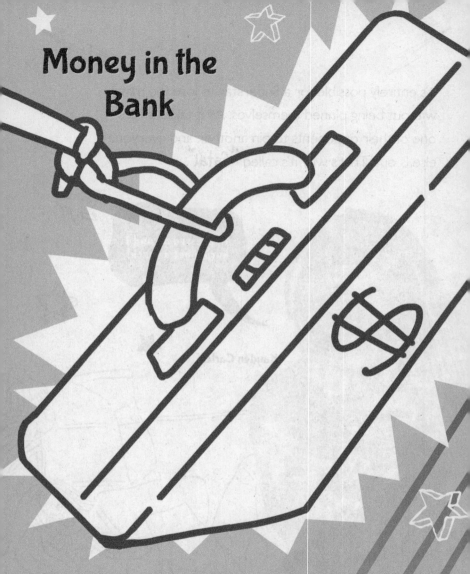

Something valuable is up for grabs in this special ladder match – quite literally. A briefcase hanging above the ring contains a **contract** that allows the Superstar who can grab it to challenge for any World Championship Match of their choosing.

The winning Superstar can **"bank"** the contract for up to one year, starting from the night they win it. If they haven't used it within the year, the contract expires. That's it. GONE.

That's mine!

Battle in the Boneyard

Only AJ Styles would be brave enough (or dumb enough) to challenge Undertaker to a Boneyard Match. He should have known that Undertaker – **aka The Deadman** – would be in his element fighting in a graveyard instead of a ring!

Undertaker

AJ Styles

AJ Styles called Undertaker "old man", and promised to bury his career. But it was AJ who got buried – in a freshly dug grave under a giant pile of earth. Undertaker ended his 21-year career on a high, riding off into the darkness on his motorcycle.

I may be older, but I still beat you AJ!

I am still phenomenal

RIP

AJ STYLES

Firefly Fun House Match

Come on in!

Somewhere in time and space exists the Firefly Fun House. In this colourful but chaotic residence, Bray **"The Fiend"** Wyatt lives – not always in harmony – with a gang of gruesome puppets.

"Pull up your pants and do the muscle man dance!"

Think you'd have fun in the Fun House? John Cena didn't! When Wyatt invited him in for a match unlike any other in WWE history, Cena was forced to relive a string of embarrassing moments from different stages in his career.

Bray Wyatt

John Cena

Swamp Match

How about ruling the swamp? You'd have to contend with mud, slime, alligators… and Bray Wyatt! Braun Strowman found out how sticky things could get when he fought Wyatt on The Fiend's home territory.

Strowman rocked up to find Wyatt relaxing in his rocking chair.

Braun Strowman

The two Superstars took the **plunge** right into the steaming, oozing, swamp. It was an Extreme Rules Match, but nobody seemed to be keeping to any rules at all.

Bray Wyatt

WWE never declared an official winner for this match. But when the bubbles cleared, it was Wyatt who surfaced with an **evil grin**.

Chamber is 8 m high (26 ft)

Plexiglass pods

Grrr... let me out!

Elimination Chamber

One ring, four pods, six Superstars... and a giant steel cage! That's what it takes to make an Elimination Chamber Match. It all starts with two Superstars in the ring and four in the pods, raring to go. Every five minutes a pod opens and another Superstar joins the fray. In the end, there should be just one Superstar left standing.

Steel ceiling

3 km (2 miles) of chain wrapped around the chamber

Black-painted frame

Any Superstar having a hard time can forget trying to escape. The steel cage around the ring prevents anyone from **climbing out**!

Hell in a Cell Matches

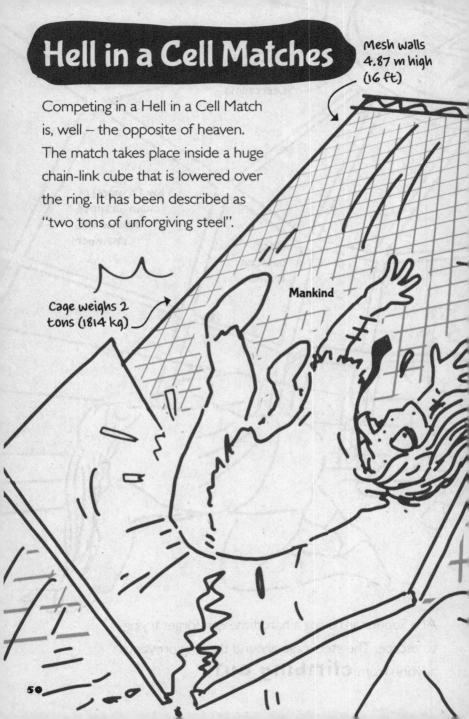

Mesh walls
4.87 m high
(16 ft)

Competing in a Hell in a Cell Match is, well – the opposite of heaven. The match takes place inside a huge chain-link cube that is lowered over the ring. It has been described as "two tons of unforgiving steel".

Cage weighs 2 tons (1814 kg)

Mankind

There aren't many rules in this thriller. Sometimes, Superstars climb the cell and fight on top of it!

Undertaker

In a famous match in 1998, Undertaker threw Mankind off the cell roof. He landed on the commentator's table, **SMASHING** it to bits.

Open-weave chain fencing

There have been a few dangerous moments when the roof has given way under a Superstar's weight. **Yikes!** To stop this happening, a new, stronger cell is now used. It's **crimson** in colour.

Hey... what gives?

Triple-Brand Chaos

The three brands

Over the years, increasing numbers of Superstars joined WWE. It all got a bit much to contain within one brand, so WWE split into three – *RAW*, *SmackDown*, and *NXT*. Each brand has its own Superstars, its own TV shows, and its own colours.

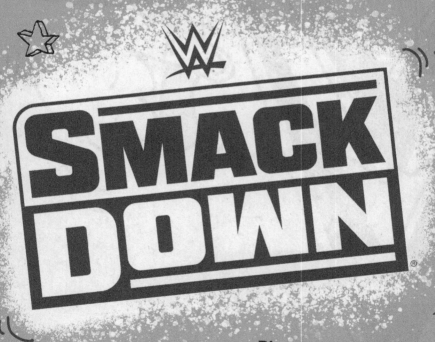

All the brand logos incorporate the **WWE logo** somewhere in their design.

Blue is the *SmackDown* colour. The original logo had an exclamation mark at the end, but it was later dropped.

RAW has a red logo with an arrow underneath. The arrow was added in **2019**.

NXT is newer than the other brands. It only started in 2010. RAW was established in 1993, while SmackDown was founded in 1999.

The NXT logo is **yellow**. Old versions had the letters arranged vertically instead of horizontally.

Brand rivalry

Each brand has its own roster of Superstars. They're all keen to compete with each other to prove their brand's dominance in WWE. Things can get a little heated in and out of the ring.

Finn Bálor

Big E

But wait… who chooses which Superstars go in which brand? That's mostly down to an **annual draft**. More about that later.

Drew McIntyre

Just to add a little excitement, something called the **BRAND-TO-BRAND INVITATION** was introduced in 2020. It allows Superstars to compete for an opposing team four times each year.

Invite

The WWE Universe

WWE fans are collectively known as the **WWE UNIVERSE**. Why Universe? Because the WWE community is absolutely huge, and like the universe it's all around us.

The WWE Universe now has a new way to watch its favourite Superstars compete under the different brands. In the **WWE THUNDERDOME**, they can grab a virtual ringside seat via live video on massive LED boards.

ThunderDome fans will be seen all over the world, so they have to respect the usual ringside rules. **Mind your language**, please, or you might be removed!

NIKKI CROSS

"THE FIEND" BRAY WYATT

ASUKA

The RAW roster

RAW's top stars include Drew McIntyre, Asuka, "The Fiend" Bray Wyatt, and a host of others.

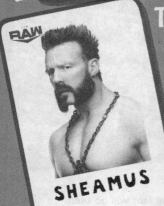

SHEAMUS

DREW McINTYRE

BOBBY LASHLEY

CHARLOTTE FLAIR

ALEXA BLISS

R-TRUTH

DREW GULAK

NAOMI

RANDY ORTON

BRAUN STROWMAN

ELIAS

DANA BROOKE

RICOCHET

The SMACKDOWN roster

Roman Reigns, Sami Zayn, Apollo Crews, and Bayley are some of the best Superstars under WWE's blue brand – SmackDown.

BAYLEY

DANIEL BRYAN

SETH ROLLINS

ROMAN REIGNS

CARMELLA

APOLLO CREWS

JEY USO

KEVIN
OWENS

MURPHY

SASHA
BANKS

OTIS

BIANCA
BELAIR

REY
MYSTERIO

BIG E

RUBY
RIOTT

FINN
BÁLOR

ADAM
COLE

RAQUEL
GONZALEZ

IO SHIRAI

The NXT roster

The Superstars of NXT are hungry up-and-comers in sports entertainment such as Adam Cole, Tommaso Ciampa, and Candice LeRae.

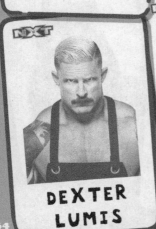

DEXTER
LUMIS

CANDICE
LERAE

SANTOS
ESCOBAR

EMBER MOON

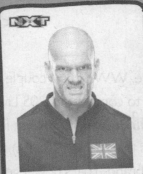

DANNY BURCH

ONEY LORCAN

ALIYAH

XIA LI

KUSHIDA

JOHNNY GARGANO

FABIAN AICHNER

TOMMASO CIAMPA

205 Live

As well as the big three, WWE has a couple of other brands for Superstars to compete in. 205 Live is for the **cruiserweights** – the smaller, lighter Superstars. You have to weigh less than 93 kg (205 lbs) to compete in this brand. That's how it gets its name, see?

If you're light you can really get some height! 205 Live is known for the high-flying action of stars such as Lucha House Party and The Brian Kendrick. (Don't forget the **"The"** in his name, by the way. He won't like that.)

NXT UK

In 2018, a new NXT brand was founded specially to showcase the talents of European Superstars. WWE quickly assembled the best in-ring competitors in Europe in NXT UK.

One of NXT UK's best Superstars is Women's Champion Kay Lee Ray. This Scottish Superstar is known for her speed, her **daredevil** dives, and her purple-red hair.

Marcel Barthel

WALTER

Fabian Aichner

Alexander Wolfe

BARTHEL
HAMBURG

AICHNER
SOUTH TYROL

Imperium is a hard-to-beat NXT UK team. It is made up of an Austrian, an Italian, and two German Superstars.

Imperium's motto is
"Die Matte ist Heilig".
That's German for "The mat is sacred".
Maybe that's why they like to give their opponents a close-up view of it!

The big events

WWE Superstars also compete in big events called **pay-per-views**. Nowadays, these events are shown on the WWE Network. The luckiest members of the WWE Universe get to watch live in the stadium. An **electric** atmosphere is guaranteed!

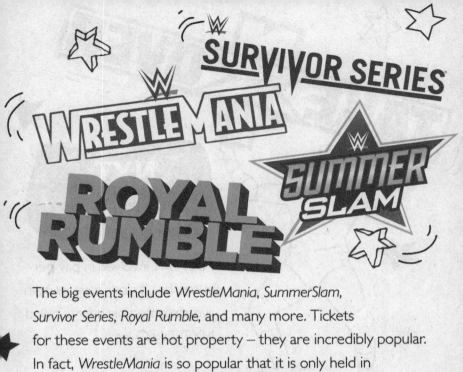

The big events include *WrestleMania*, *SummerSlam*, *Survivor Series*, *Royal Rumble*, and many more. Tickets for these events are hot property — they are incredibly popular. In fact, *WrestleMania* is so popular that it is only held in stadiums that can seat at least 70,000.

TAKE NXT OVER

NXT TakeOver

NXT isn't involved in pay-per-views, but it does have its own live-streamed big events called NXT TakeOver.

TAKE NXT UK OVER

The Viking Raiders

They might be held on their own, or on the same weekend as a WWE pay-per-view, in the same city, and sometimes in the same venue.

NXT TakeOver events aren't meant to take attention away from the pay-per-views. They're intended to **support** them.

Shayna Baszler

Asuka

The WWE Universe just can't get enough, so why not give them **more, more, more?**

Talk, talk, talk

Have you got the gift of the gab? Most Superstars are only too happy to give their jaw muscles a workout on **RAW Talk**, **Talking Smack**, and **The Bump**. WWE's TV talk shows feature breaking news and Superstar interviews that just can't be seen anywhere else.

He can be a real fiend. I'm gonna make him pay for what he did to me!

Kayla Braxton

Xavier Woods

Roman Reigns

Sometimes, a Superstar's remarks are intended for their rivals as much as for the fans. It's one surefire way to get their **attention**!

Does he mean me?

Bray Wyatt

Go with the stream

Perhaps the best place to catch all the WWE action is on WWE Network.

This 24-hour streaming service brings news, interviews, and matches to millions of viewers from nearly two hundred countries around the world.

Subscribers can watch every pay-per-view match in history, exclusive in-ring action, documentaries, reality shows, replays, and more. **Phew... that's a whole lot of viewing!**

superstar
stories

Roman Reigns

Tattoo covers entire arm and shoulder

Roman Reigns is from the **Anoa'i family** – a long line of WWE Superstars. He's carried on their legacy on by winning several WWE and Universal Championships.

Personalised cuffs

The Shield's team logo.

Reigns calls himself **"The Big Dog"**, and says WWE is his "yard". That's not just talk. Many Superstars have learned that the Big Dog's bite is as bad as his bark, in a variety of painful ways.

The Spear is Reigns' signature move. He runs at his opponent, launches himself horizontally at them, and **KNOCKS** them down to the mat.

Drew McIntyre

Drew McIntyre is the first Scottish-born WWE Champion. He beat Brock Lesnar to take the Title at *WrestleMania 36* in 2020.

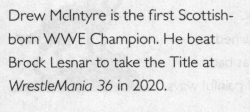

Drew has a masters degree in criminology

Just months earlier, McIntyre was last man standing in the **30-man** Royal Rumble Match.

"Talk less, clay more"

"Talk Less, Clay More" is the 1.96m (6 ft 5 in) Scot's motto. What's that all about? Well, a claymore is the name of a traditional Scottish sword but also of McIntyre's signature kick. It's a **flying mid–air kick** with both feet forward. He claims he invented it in a match when his shorts were so tight he couldn't kick in the normal way!

McIntyre has two cats, known as the **claymore cats**. Their favourite toy is his WWE title!

Bayley

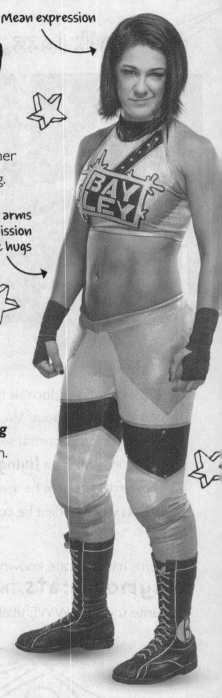

Mean expression

Bayley was once known for her friendly, colourful image. **"I'm a Hugger"** was her motto, and she was always smiling.

Strong arms for submission holds, not hugs

Now she's **more aggressive**, and her career has gone from strength to strength.

She became the *longest-reigning* SmackDown Women's Champion.

When Bayley decided to get tough, she **chopped off** her trademark side ponytail.

Then she chopped down the inflatable tube men that used to accompany her as she walked to the ring. They were a part of the playful image she wanted to leave behind.

Bayley is keen to be an inspiration to girls. Her new motto is "I'm a Role Model."

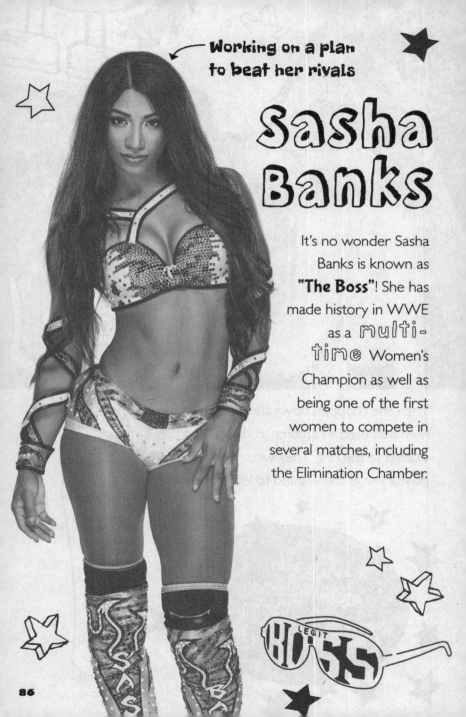

Working on a plan to beat her rivals

Sasha Banks

It's no wonder Sasha Banks is known as **"The Boss"**! She has made history in WWE as a multi-time Women's Champion as well as being one of the first women to compete in several matches, including the Elimination Chamber.

For a long time, Sasha was in a tag team partnership with Bayley. But at *WrestleMania 36*, their competitive instincts boiled over and they fell out. Now, Sasha considers Bayley to be her **greatest rival**.

She likes nothing better than to take down her ex-partner with her signature move— the Bank Statement.

The Bank Statement involves pulling back on her opponent's upper body.

The New Day

Xavier Woods

Big E

Kofi Kingston

The New Day are a tag team who bring the power of **positivity** to every match. This upbeat trio wear **BRIGHTLY COLOURED** stage gear, and often begin or end their appearances by **bursting** into dance or song.

They held the Tag Team Title for l o n g e r than anyone else in WWE history, reigning for an amazing

Oh, come on... let someone else have a turn...

483 days

between **2015** and **2017**.

Woods' beloved trombone, named

Francesca,

is sometimes referred to as the fourth member of the team.

When the **New Day** dismiss an opponent as "booty!" they are calling them **UNCOOL**. But there's nothing uncool about **Booty-O's**, the team's very own brand of cereal.

The New Day's signature move is the

Midnight Hour.

Big E hoists an opponent onto his shoulder, and Kingston or Woods leaps off the ropes to **slam** him down to the mat.

Braun Strowman

They call Braun Strowman "The Monster Among Men".

That's because he's

HUGE

in size, *IMMENSE* in strength, and shows absolutely **no mercy** to his opponents.

Strowman was the "Black Sheep" of The Wyatt family

Strowman isn't even picky about keeping the fight in the ring. He once **overturned an ambulance** because he knew Roman Reigns was inside.

Well this got turned on its head

Strowman started out as a member of **The Wyatt Family**, Bray Wyatt's faction. However, they had a disagreement.

When a Superstar family fall out, things can get **really, really bad**.

Bray Wyatt

Huskus The Pig Boy

Abby The Witch

Bray Wyatt had a dark alter ego named the "**The Fiend**", who sought revenge on all those who had harmed Bray. Thankfully, he's gone now, and Bray wants to be a friend, **not a fiend**

He even presents a kids' TV show called **Firefly Fun House**. It's a bright and happy home – until The Fiend starts to take over again…

Yowie Wowie! We're gonna have so much fun here...

Ramblin' Rabbit

Mercy The Buzzard

It only takes a bad memory or a careless word from a puppet to bring The Fiend back!

AJ Styles

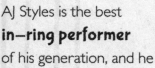

AJ Styles is the best **in-ring performer** of his generation, and he doesn't mind telling you!

Long, flowing hair

Vest hides tattoo of his initials

Always wears gloves

Well, it isn't exactly modest to call *SmackDown* **"the house that AJ built"**. Fortunately, the **"Phenomenal One"** has the phenomenal skills to back up his confidence!

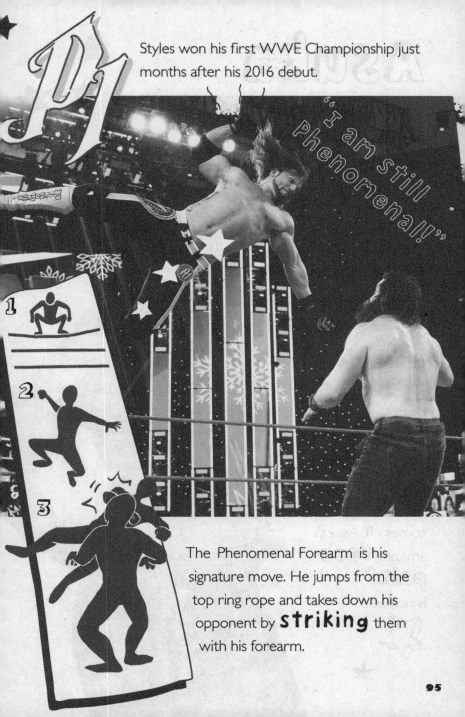

Styles won his first WWE Championship just months after his 2016 debut.

"I am still Phenomenal!"

The Phenomenal Forearm is his signature move. He jumps from the top ring rope and takes down his opponent by **striking** them with his forearm.

Asuka

She calls herself **"The Empress of Tomorrow"**, but Asuka is doing pretty well for herself today. Famous for her multicoloured costumes and hair, her menacing grin, and her masks, Asuka was **undefeated** for more than two years. She's still almost impossible to beat!

Warrior face paint

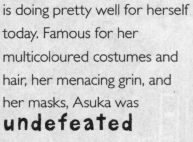

When the mask comes off, Asuka's amazing **face paint** is revealed.

Asuka's masks are based on those worn in
Japanese Noh theatre.

Asuka's legs wrap around
Ember Moon's waist

Ember Moon cannot move

Don't get locked in! When the Empress of Tomorrow
uses the **Asuka Lock** manoeuvre, she wraps her
arms and legs around her opponent from behind. Usually,
the only way out is to **tap out!**

The Road to WrestleMania

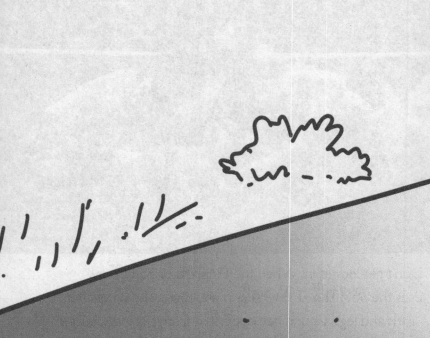

Daniel Bryan after defeating Batista and Randy Orton, WrestleMania 30

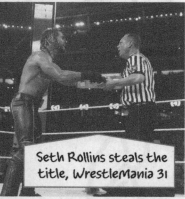

Seth Rollins steals the title, WrestleMania 31

Andre the Giant vs Hulk Hogan, WrestleMania 3

The history of *WrestleMania*

The first ever *WrestleMania* took place in 1985 in Madison Square Garden, New York City. It was the brainchild of WWE owner **Mr. Mc Mahon**. He thought fans would love a spectacular where they could see all kinds of Superstars in all kinds of matches. He was right! Today, *WrestleMania* is the biggest annual event in WWE. It's always full of incredible, memorable **"WrestleMania Moments"**.

Shawn Michaels vs Razor Ramon, WrestleMania X

Shawn Michaels vs Ric Flair, WrestleMania 24

Undertaker buries AJ Styles, WrestleMania 36

Royal Rumble Matches

What's the first step on the road to *WrestleMania*?
Well, it all begins with a Royal Rumble Match,
where **30** Superstars compete for a Championship
opportunity at *WrestleMania*. Their aim is to
𝕥𝕙𝕣𝕠𝕨 their rivals out of the ring.

Take your pick!

Decision, decisions! The winners of the men's and women's Royal Rumble Matches get to pick their opponent for a Title Match at *WrestleMania*. They might pick an old foe, a cocky young upstart, or someone on an amazing run of victories.

I challenge Brock Lesnar!

Drew McIntyre ended Brock Lesnar's **13-win run** in a Royal Rumble Match. He didn't waste a moment in picking Lesnar again to battle for the WWE Title at *WrestleMania*.

Some Superstars **REALLY, REALLY** want to be picked.

Do you REALLY wanna do this?

Rhea Ripley actually demanded that **10-time world champion** Charlotte Flair pick her for a match at *WrestleMania 36*! (She might have regretted it by the end of the match, when she was forced to tap out.)

Just sign here...

Big matches require both contestants to sign a contract, right there in the middle of the ring. That should be a nice, civilised affair, right? **WRONG!** Contract signings for *WrestleMania* matches often break down into **chaos**.

When Superstars share the ring to sign a contract, someone usually ends up being **slammed through a table**!

A manager, director, or other official must be present to oversee the contract signing. Sometimes it's another Superstar, or an ex-Superstar. They bring the contract into the ring in a black folder.

Axxess all areas

WrestleMania Axxess is an annual **four-day** fan convention. Held the week before *WrestleMania*, it gives the WWE Universe an opportunity to watch live matches, enjoy once-in-a-lifetime WWE experiences, and take home memorable merchandise.

WWE SHOP

Awesome, it's Randy Orton!

Me next, Randy!

Sure thing!

Can you sign this, sir?

RKO

One of the biggest attractions for fans is the chance to meet their favourite Superstars.

The first WrestleMania Axxess was held in 1988 for WrestleMania IV. It was quite a small gathering then. Today, it's huge!

Something else **HUGE** is the statue of Andre the Giant which featured at WrestleMania Axxess 2013. It's a tradition to unveil a bronze statue of a different WWE Hall of Famer every year at the event.

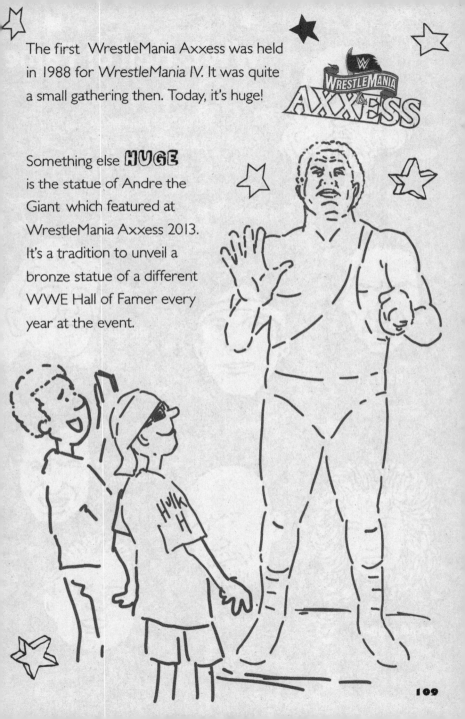

Big John Studd

WWE Hall of Fame

If you're good enough to become a legend amongst Superstars, you might… just might… make it into the **WWE Hall of Fame**. WWE inducts a new class of Superstars every year during *WrestleMania* week.

Booker T

Ricky Steamboat

Ric Flair

Gorilla Monsoon

Wendi Richter

Stone Cold Steve Austin

The British Bulldog

The Ultimate Warrior

Bret "Hit Man" Hart

Randy Savage

Goldberg

 Here are a some of the 2020-2021 Hall of Famers.

Batista

The Bella Twins

JBL

NWO

X-Pac

Hulk Hogan

Kevin Nash

Scott Hall

111

Pageantry

Fanfare, dazzle, razzmatazz, and glitz -- *WrestleMania* brings fans all these things as well as in-ring action! That's why it's known as "The Show of Shows".

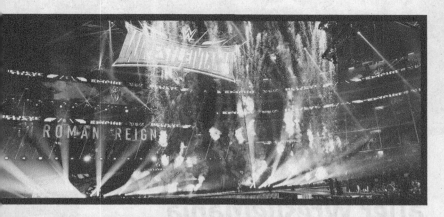

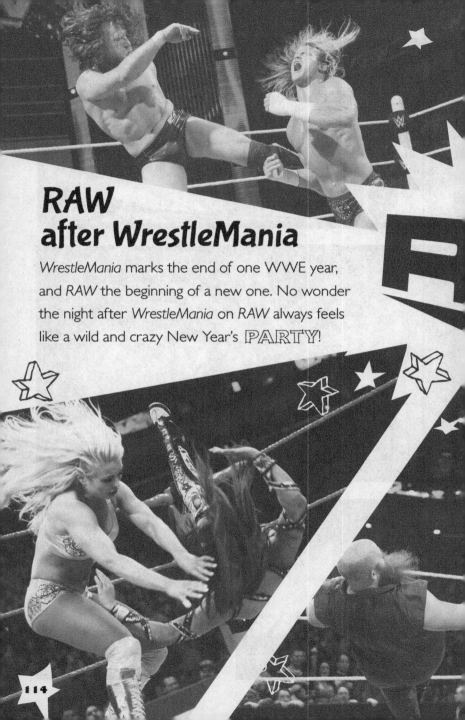

RAW
after WrestleMania

WrestleMania marks the end of one WWE year, and *RAW* the beginning of a new one. No wonder the night after *WrestleMania* on *RAW* always feels like a wild and crazy New Year's PARTY!

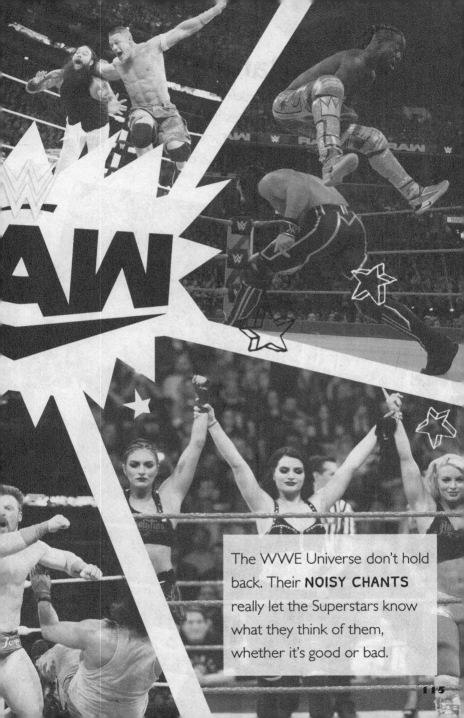

The WWE Universe don't hold back. Their **NOISY CHANTS** really let the Superstars know what they think of them, whether it's good or bad.

The Superstar Shakeup

In the weeks following *WrestleMania*, every Superstar waits to discover their new destiny in the Superstar Shakeup, sometimes known as just The Draft. It might – or might not – send a Superstar from their current brand to a **NEW** one.

Once in a brand, most Superstars are very, very loyal. At least until next year...

Welcome to RAW, AJ Styles!

It's sad, but sometimes a team gets *split up*. In 2020, that happened to The New Day. Kofi Kingston and Xavier Woods were sent to *RAW*, and Big E went to *SmackDown!*

... See you next time!

A true Superstar keeps pushing forward. Whether they've had a good or a bad year, there's no time to dwell on the past. What they need is to get planning for the future. **ONWARD!**

WrestleMania next year!

Apollo Crews

As soon as *WrestleMania* is over, the WWE Superstars start looking ahead to next year's event. **championship gold** is already on their minds. And with new faces jostling with old, everything is up for grabs...

Chelsea Green

Do you have what it takes?

By now you know pretty much everything about WWE.

You know the **brands**.

You've met some of the biggest **Superstars**.

Shayna Baszler

Undertaker

Roman Reigns

John Cena

Keith Lee

Bray Wyatt

Asuka

So how about it? Do you think you could **RULE THE RING**?

Glossary

Athlete
A person who is skilled at a sport.

Catchphrase
A phrase or saying that is often repeated.

Competitor
Someone a Superstar battles in a contest.

Elimination Chamber
An event where competitors attempt to escape a large cage.

Iron Man Match
A contest where competitors must get the most pins within a set time, usually 30 or 60 minutes.

Opponent
Someone who competes against another person in a contest.

2 out of 3 Falls Match
A match where an individual or team must get two pins, submissions, or knockouts in order to win the match.

No Holds Barred Match
A match where competitors cannot be disqualified for breaking the rules.

"I Quit" Match

A match where competitors battle until one submits and says "I quit".

Backstage Brawl

A match-up that takes place outisde of the ring, backstage.

Pay-per-view

A special lineup of matches that can be viewed on television for an extra fee.

Pin

A competitor covers an opponent and holds their shoulders down while a referee counts to three and pounds the mat three times.

Referee

A person who oversees a match and makes sure rules are followed.

Roster

All the Superstars who fight under one of WWE's brands: *RAW*, *SmackDown*, or *NXT*.

Signature move

A Superstar's best move in the ring. Superstars perfect their signature moves and give them interesting names.

WWE ThunderDome

An arena where matches are held. It can also accommodate video conferencing for large crowds.

Index

Index continued

Project Editor Pamela Afram
Senior Designer Nathan Martin
Senior Production Editor Marc Staples
Senior Production Controller Louise Minihane
Managing Editor Sarah Harland
Managing Art Editor Vicky Short
Publishing Director Mark Searle

Design and illustrations by Guy Harvey
DK would like to thank Jake Black for his editorial assistance.

First published in Great Britain in 2021
by Dorling Kindersley Limited
DK, One Embassy Gardens,
8 Viaduct Gardens, London SW11 7BW

The authorised representative in the EEA is
Dorling Kindersley Verlag GmbH. Arnulfstr.
124, 80636 Munich, Germany

Page design copyright © 2021 Dorling
Kindersley Limited

10 9 8 7 6 5 4 3
003–321710–Jul/2021

A CIP catalogue record for this book
is available from the British Library.

ISBN 978-0-24146-760-2

Printed and bound in the UK

For the curious

www.dk.com
www.wwe.com

MIX
Paper from
responsible sources
FSC™ C018179

This book is made from
Forest Stewardship Council™
certified paper – one small
step in DK's commitment
to a sustainable future.